Foreword

The 1949 decision to sink HMS *Implacable* - the last wooden 'ship of the line' then still afloat and the only French survivor of the Battle of Trafalgar - was a negative but important event in the modern development of historic ship preservation. It was also a moment of truth for the young National Maritime Museum, which played a significant though unsuccessful part in the efforts to save *Implacable*. Sadly, however, her rapidly deteriorating condition during the Second World War and the harsh economic climate afterwards made this impossible.

In December that year, after her Medusa figurehead and most of her stern decoration were removed for the Museum, the old ship was scuttled with full naval honours in the English Channel. While her figurehead has since glowered over generations of visitors to Greenwich, the rest has spent the last half century boxed-up in our stores, awaiting an opportunity to see the light of a new day.

We are all delighted that, after some false dawns in the last fifty years, this day has now arrived. Thanks to the generosity of our Danish friends at Hempel's Marine Paints, the reconstructed stern of *Implacable,* with her figurehead, finally look out over the heart of the Museum - itself also now fully reconstructed to greet the 21st century.

It is many years since *Implacable*'s fascinating story appeared in print and it never has done in a well illustrated form. We are very grateful to Hempel's, both for their part in the physical reconstruction of the ship's stern in the Museum's new Neptune Court and for supporting publication of this account of the life, death - and now partial resurrection - of 'the last of the 74s'.

Richard Ormond

Richard Ormond
Director
National Maritime Museum, Greenwich

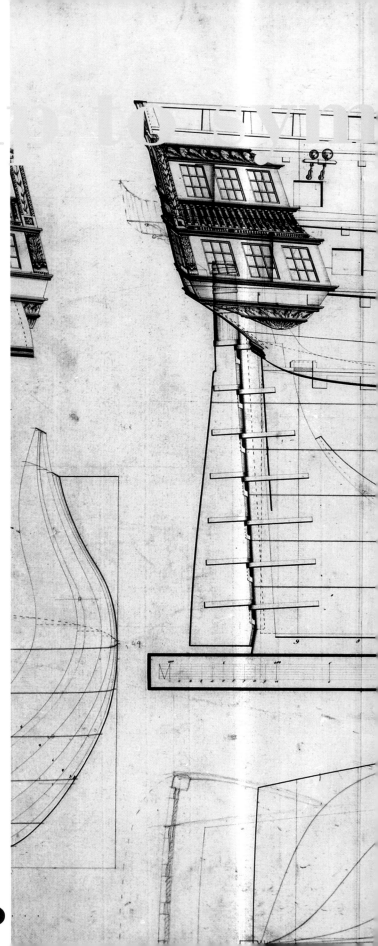

From ship to symbol

On 4 November 1805 four French warships heading for the safety of Rochefort, on France's Atlantic coast, were intercepted by a Royal Naval squadron under the command of Admiral Sir Richard Strachan. It was a fortnight after the Battle of Trafalgar, in which a combined Franco-Spanish force had been decisively defeated by the British fleet. One of the French commanders, Rear-Admiral Dumanoir Le Pelley, had managed to escape in his flagship *Formidable*, accompanied by the *Scipion*, *Mont Blanc* and *Duguay-Trouin*, but had fallen foul of Strachan's patrol on 2 November. For two days the British pursued them until, in a brief but murderous engagement, Dumanoir's ships were one-by-one forced by a numerically superior enemy to strike their colours. Taken in tow, they were brought to Plymouth as prizes and after refitting were absorbed into the Royal Navy.

The *Duguay-Trouin* was renamed *Implacable*. She became in turn a Royal Naval ship of the line, a naval training ship, a training vessel for Sea Scouts, a holiday ship for working-class boys and girls, and a war-time transport and bulk-carrier. In 1949 she was scuttled with full naval honours by the Admiralty. Yet even this produced another metamorphosis, for her destruction was so widely regretted that she became the symbol for the World Ship Trust, formed in 1979, whose badge still bears the image of the ship's stern and the motto '*Implacable*, Never Again'.

Meanwhile, the *Implacable*'s figurehead - a representation of Medusa - and the original ornamental stern carvings, both of which were removed prior to her destruction, have been placed on display in the National Maritime Museum, Greenwich, the costs of the project being borne by the Heritage Lottery Fund and Hempel's Marine Paints, Denmark. In these pages we trace *Implacable*'s career and her legacy.

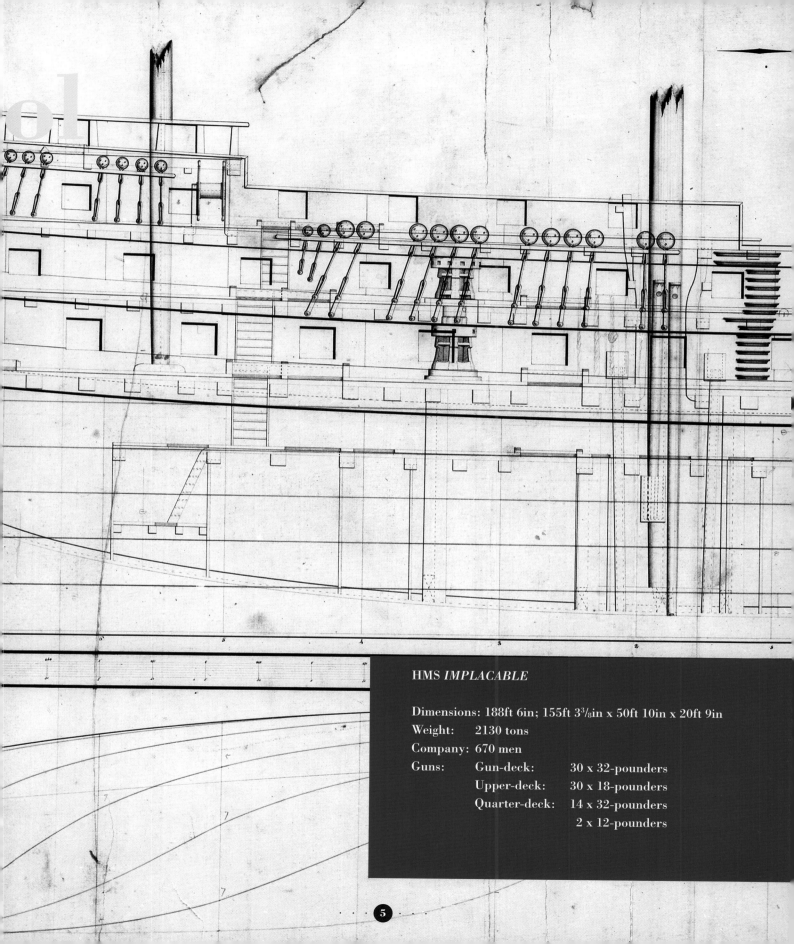

HMS *IMPLACABLE*

Dimensions: 188ft 6in; 155ft 3³⁄₈in x 50ft 10in x 20ft 9in
Weight: 2130 tons
Company: 670 men
Guns: Gun-deck: 30 x 32-pounders
           Upper-deck: 30 x 18-pounders
           Quarter-deck: 14 x 32-pounders
                          2 x 12-pounders

The ship of war

Laid down in Rochefort in 1797 and launched in 1800, the 74-gun *Duguay-Trouin* was named after one of France's most celebrated naval commanders René Duguay-Trouin (1673-1736). Born in St. Malô to a seafaring family his first war service came in 1689 during France's protracted struggle against England and Holland, when at the age of 16 he shipped aboard a privateer equipped by his father. By 1691 the young René had his first command, the 14-gun frigate *Danycarn*, also fitted out by his family. In the same year, driven by storms upon the west coast of Ireland, he sailed up the River Limerick where he set fire to two British ships and several houses before escaping pursued by a detachment of troops from Limerick Castle. Between 1692 and 1696 Duguay-Trouin, promoted to the command of larger ships, consolidated his reputation as a daring and resourceful commander. He harried enemy merchantmen and warships, escaped from imprisonment in Plymouth and from 1694 served with the La Rochelle squadron. In 1696 he was given his first commission as a commander in the French navy. Along with other *corsaires* he became a key figure in Louis XIV's fleet, and in 1728 he was appointed Lieutenant-Général des Armées Navales.

Over 70 years later the warship *Duguay-Trouin* took her place in a fleet serving a republican government rather than a feudal monarchy. War, however, remained a constant and control of the seas the key to victory, as the nations of a divided Europe fought to defend not only their home territories but also their distant colonies. Joining the squadron of Rear Admiral Dumanoir in 1805 the *Duguay-Trouin*, under Captain Claude Touffet, saw action in the final stages of the Battle of Trafalgar, at one point engaging Admiral

René Duguay-Trouin, Lieutenant-Général des Armées Navales (1673-1736)

Nelson's flagship *Victory*. But her late intervention made little difference to the outcome. As defeat loomed Dumanoir's squadron headed southward, a flight which took Touffet to his death and the *Duguay-Trouin*, like her famous namesake, to Plymouth.

In 1806 a refitted *Duguay-Trouin* was renamed HMS *Implacable* and taken into the Royal Navy establishment as a 'third-rate'. The term has now come to mean sub-standard but it simply referred to her size: ships of 100 guns or more were first-rates, those of 90 'second', those of 64 to 84 'third-rates' - all fit to lie in the line of battle, opposed to enemy ships of similar size.

As the war dragged on, *Implacable*, with a full complement of 670 men, including soldiers and marines, now sailed out to fight the French and their allies. In 1808-09 as part of a Baltic expedition in support of Britain's ally Sweden, she distinguished herself in engagements against the combined forces of Denmark and Russia in the Bay of Hangö, where she seized and destroyed the Russian *Sevolod* (see illustration overleaf), and in the Barö Sound off the coast of Finland. However, after Bonaparte's defeat in 1815 the Royal Navy's role was largely that of peacekeeping in the huge and rapidly expanding territory of the British empire.

Implacable next saw action in 1840 off the coast of Syria against an Egyptian fleet trained and officered by the French navy and fighting for independence from Turkey, at that time one of Britain's allies. But this was her last major engagement. In 1842, having been voted the smartest ship in the Mediterranean fleet, she sailed home to Plymouth where she was paid off. She never again fired her guns in anger.

*The Battle of Trafalgar by J. M W. Turner (1775-1851).
The battle, fought on 21 October 1805 off the south-west
coast of Spain, has inspired numerous paintings,
Turner's focusing on Nelson's flagship Victory. This
imaginative reconstruction, displayed in the Naval
Gallery at Greenwich Hospital during the nineteenth century, was tremendously popular with the public but much de-
rided by seafarers who complained of its many inaccura-
cies.*

*The victor of Trafalgar,
Vice-Admiral Lord Nelson (1758-1805).
This painting by Lemuel Abbott (1760-1803)
dates to the Battle of the Nile in 1798 when Nelson was
aged 40. Mortally wounded at Trafalgar by a sniper's
bullet, he died as the news came of the enemy's defeat.*

❦ The wind was too scant to effect this desirable object, and after keeping the ship very close to the wind to try it, she was edged away and passed a few feet from the lee quarter of the enemy, when a broadside with three shot in every gun (except the carronades which had only one) was poured into her with tremendous effect, and the two ships continued abreast of each other for a time, but unfortunately the *Implacable* forged ahead more than was desirable although the sails were backed to prevent it: she presently recovered from her position abreast of the enemy and our fire seemed to tear the ship to pieces.

The Russian had the ensign twice shot away and finally hauled down the pendant in token of surrender. At this time the whole Russian fleet was coming down upon us before the wind, and the advanced ship a three-decker not far off: and the *Centaur* having our signal up to discontinue the action. and the of recall and the boats which were ordered to be lowered to take possession of the enemy having been damaged in the action. I was constrained to abandon a ship so completely beaten and bore up to close the Admiral. On closing with the *Centaur* she gave us three cheers and I had the gratification to meet the most cordial reception from Sir Samuel Hood with the warmest expressions of approbation of what he had witnessed. ❧

Captain Thomas Byam Martin
HMS *Implacable*
Baltic, 26 August 1808, off Hangö Head

The Capture of the *Sevolod; oil painting by Johannes E. Møller, 1999*

*I*mplacable was retained 'in ordinary', performing various tasks and harbour duties in Plymouth. In June 1853 tension between Russia and Turkey saw the fleet ordered to the Dardanelles, to be joined there by the French navy as a prelude to the Crimean War (1853-56), but the *Implacable* did not go. Instead, in 1855, she was designated as a training ship for naval cadets, taking on boys of 15 to 18 to prepare them for service at sea.

The Royal Navy had introduced formal practical training only the year before, with the establishment at Portsmouth of the training ship *Illustrious*. From the 1870s training was carried out mainly in shore-based establishments with ships in attendance. In 1871, reflecting this change, the *Implacable* was taken into the *Lion* training establishment, Devonport. By the 1890s however, even though the number of training vessels world-wide was growing, the Royal Navy was beginning to question their usefulness in an age of steam which required seafarers to have scientific and technical skills.

Implacable survived as a training ship into the 1900s but in 1902 sail-training was abolished in the Royal Navy and in 1904 the ship was decommissioned and offered for sale.

All present and correct.
Naval cadets undergoing training in the Lion,
with officers and instructors, 1899.
Navy and Army Illustrated, *5 August 1899.*

Left: **Sail drill.**
Cadets aloft on the Lion, *at Devonport,*
with the Implacable *moored astern, about 1900.*

The Trafalgar vet

The Trafalgar veteran

By 1904 HMS *Implacable*, moored at Devonport, and HMS *Victory*, still used for harbour duties at Portsmouth, were the only surviving ships from the Battle of Trafalgar. They also represented a dwindling number of wooden warships generally, as the world's maritime nations were increasingly caught up in a naval arms race to equip national fleets with modern ships of iron and steel, powered by steam. In these competitive conditions obsolete vessels were increasingly likely to be disposed of.

The idea that such ships had historical significance and might in some way be preserved was not unknown but tended to surface infrequently. HMS *Victory*, for example, was condemned to be broken up in 1816 but was saved by a campaign in the press which invoked the memory of Nelson and the sacrifice of those who fell with him at Trafalgar. Given special moorings, she became the flagship of the Commander-in-Chief, Portsmouth, in 1825.

In the USA, in 1828, a similar process led to a reprieve for the USS *Constitution*, a veteran of the War of 1812 against Britain. By 1858 this frigate, known as 'Old Ironsides', was designated as a training ship for the US Naval Academy, Annapolis (established in 1849). In both these cases, however, although public opinion had led to the ships being saved, it was state money channelled through naval budgets which ensured their continued survival by paying for their ever-necessary maintenance.

From the 1890s the issue of preservation began to surface more frequently. Interest in historic ships was boosted both by the decline of wooden sailing vessels and by the rise of nationalism, which on occasions used old as well as new ships to symbolise the continuity of national maritime prowess. Yet the problems of preservation remained.

A section of public opinion, especially former seafarers, yachtsmen, and naval historians, tended to argue that the state had a moral responsibility towards vessels which had not only served the country but had also become part of the fabric of national history. Government departments, on the other hand, although increasingly ready to subsidise ancient buildings and monuments, were loath to fund ship projects, especially at a time when naval budgets were spiralling.

Between these extremes the general public, although sympathetic to the idea of rescuing old ships, could not be counted on to donate money when appeals were made. In 1904 the selling-off of the *Implacable* illustrated the problems.

When the intended disposal of the ship was made public Geoffrey Wheatly Cobb (1851-1931), a wealthy industrialist living in South Wales, requested the Admiralty to postpone the sale until he could raise the purchase price. Cobb had been a thorn in the Admiralty's side since the 1890s, berating their Lordships for the sale of 'England's wooden walls' and making public the fact that in 1892 the *Foudroy-*

Sail and steam.
Implacable *under tow, probably to Falmouth, in 1927.*

Opposite page: Restoration under way.
Implacable *in dry-dock, August 1925. As well as showing the decorated stern, the photograph illustrates the immense size of the ship and the considerable proportion which was usually below the waterline.*

ant, briefly Nelson's flagship in 1799, had been sold to a German shipbreaker's yard.

Cobb's campaign to repatriate the *Foudroyant* whipped up xenophopbia but a subsequent public appeal to rescue the ship failed to raise hard cash. Ultimately the *Foudroyant* was purchased from Germany by a business syndicate, which intended to exhibit her on the Thames but eventually went bankrupt. Cobb took the ship over at his and his father's expense, recruiting a crew of young boys and sailing the *Foudroyant* to ports around Britain as an 'exhibition ship' until she was wrecked near Blackpool in 1897.

Later that year he spent £1,323 buying the frigate *Trincomalee*, a fifth-rate launched in 1817, which he renamed *Foudroyant*. This ship, with the exhortation 'Remember Nelson' inscribed by Cobb on the break of her quarter-deck, was initially moored at Cowes. In 1904, after disputes over moorings, he had her towed to Falmouth, then Milford Haven. In 1904 when he applied to purchase the *Implacable* he made it clear that he wished to use her as a training vessel with the *Trincomalee/ Foudroyant*.

Cobb's wealth came from his family's investments in coal and other industrial and commercial ventures in Wales. In the 1830s his grandparents had moved from Oxfordshire to Wales, where his father, Joseph Richard Cobb (1821-97), a keen antiquarian, carried out a good deal of the restoration of the castles at Pembroke and Manorbier. In 1884 he purchased and restored Caldicot Castle, near Chepstow, which was used as the family home. When in 1904 attempts to ignite public interest in the *Implacable* failed, and the Admiralty put the ship back on the market, Geoffrey Cobb made an

appeal to King Edward VII who intervened to halt the sale. This impasse continued for several years. In 1909 Cobb, when a guest at a Royal Academy banquet, circulated a petition to be sent to the First Lord of the Admiralty, requesting the loan of the vessel for use as a training ship in Falmouth, where the *Foudroyant* had been permanently moored since 1905.

Cobb received support from Royal Academicians such as John Singer Sargent, Sir Lawrence Alma-Tadema and William Lionel Wyllie, and their guests including Rudyard Kipling and W. S. Gilbert, all of whom signed the petition which called for the reprieve of *Implacable* 'as a monument to the brave men of 1805'. The sale continued to be delayed but after a further three years' negotiation Cobb acquired *Implacable* on loan as a training ship and in 1912 she sailed for Falmouth harbour.

The stern galleries of the Implacable *after the second restoration in 1936.*

Geoffrey Wheatly Cobb.

Afloat again, 1927.
Taken after the completion in 1927 of the first major restoration; again, possibly en route to Falmouth.

Living quarters.
The Cobbs entertained their guests in some style, inviting them to Falmouth and giving them the option of staying ashore or afloat. Admiral Doveton Sturdee was one of those who chose to sleep on board ship. The photograph of one of Foudroyant's stern cabins suggests that the state rooms were furnished in the style of a country house, with a touch of the Raj.

The adventure ship

A ided by donations, again principally from his family, Cobb began to fit out the *Implacable*. Reminiscing in the 1980s of his days on the training ship as a boy of 13, Ted Johns of Manorbier recalled that he and his fellow trainees were kitted out with uniforms, given bed and board, and pay of 2s.6d. a week. There were usually about twenty-six boys and young men on board, with occasional visits from other groups. As well as learning the basics of seamanship the crew also formed rowing, football and cricket teams, and a ship's band. They received a month's holiday a year, and at Christmas the 'best' of them would be invited by Cobb to Caldicot Castle.

During the First World War, however, although the training continued there was little opportunity to carry out maintenance. By 1918 the teak-built *Trincomalee* was still in good repair but the *Implacable*, with its 'heart of oak', was in need of urgent attention. In 1920 the Admiralty, which still owned the ship, informed Cobb that unless he had her repaired she would have to be surrendered for destruction. Cobb pleaded poverty, caused by post-war rises in taxation and the annual costs of running the training establishment, which he estimated at £5,000. The Admiralty, doing its best to assist, offered to take the *Implacable* to Devonport, repair her and return her to Falmouth at a total cost of £6,180.

The debate on the *Implacable* in 1920 ushered in yet another world-wide surge of interest in old sailing ships as enthusiasts sought not only to save the 'last of the line' but also to rebuild the world they had known before the First World War. Historic ships were increasingly becoming public exhibits, either in their own right or as part of larger open-air maritime sites. In 1922 Wilfred Dowman, a retired merchant navy officer, purchased the former tea clipper *Cutty Sark*, fitting her out as a training vessel in Falmouth and showing her off by sailing her to the Isle of Wight during Cowes Week in 1924.

Both the *Victory* and the *Constitution* underwent major repairs and preservation. The Portsmouth venture was funded jointly by the Admiralty and the Society for Nautical Research (SNR); the Boston project was financed by the American people, after Congress ordered repairs but voted that the money had to be raised by public

All hands on deck.
Sea Scouts on Foudroyant; *probably taken in the 1920s. This is reproduced from an album of photographs of life on board the* Implacable *and* Foudroyant, *in the Museum's collections.*

appeal. There were moves towards forming new museums in which sailing craft were central features. Where old ships were lacking, relatively recent ones could be preserved, as in 1926 in Japan where the British-built battleship *Mikasa* (1900) - which had been Admiral Togo's flagship in the Russo-Japanese war of 1904-5 - was made into a naval memorial.

In this period Cobb again played a pioneering role. Searching for financial backing in 1920 he turned to Sir Robert Baden-Powell, founder of the Boy Scout movement. In 1909 Baden-Powell had contacted Cobb asking if he might bring a hundred Sea Scouts to Falmouth for a short course of naval instruction.

As the *Trincomalee* was only a small ship Cobb had to refuse but he was able to take small groups for short adventure holidays, a scheme which proved popular with the Sea Scouts. He now contacted Baden-Powell, suggesting that the Scout Association might take over the *Implacable* as a Sea Scout headquarters and training centre. With Baden-Powell's agreement Cobb wrote to *The Times* announcing this plan and appealing for £10,000 to repair and refit the ship to take 250 boys. He also called on the public to remember the work done by the Scouts during the war, when they had assisted the coastguard in watching for enemy shipping. At this stage several of Cobb's 'influential friends' - they remain anonymous - offered to donate money to the cause on condition that a fund of £20,000 was raised and invested to secure permanent income for the ship. The scheme was launched on 15 January 1921, with the Prince of Wales - who was also Chief Scout for Wales - appealing for the considerable sum of £200,000 to enable the Scout Association to continue and expand its activities, and to set up the *Implacable* as a Sea Scout training ship.

Although the scheme raised a good deal of money there was not enough to guarantee the proposed *Implacable* fund. Cobb continued to take parties of scouts, Navy League cadets and others for training on his ships, but it was clearly becoming beyond his capabilities and his means. In 1921, aged 70, he married Anna Beach, a wealthy woman whose pursuit of the bachelor Cobb included having her half-timbered Sussex home dismantled and re-erected in Falmouth, overlooking *Implacable*'s moorings. By the mid-1920s however, the couple were once again looking for sponsors. In

Opposite page:
Taking a dip.
The sail-training ethos was intended to encourage self-reliance and physical stamina. Here Sea Scouts enjoy, or endure, a swim in Falmouth harbour, with life-boats at hand.

1924 they rented out Caldicot Castle and moved permanently to Falmouth. Cobb, placing a letter in *The Times* in April, observed that the renting of the castle represented 'the last sacrifice to preserve the *Implacable*', which was once again under threat of being broken up by the Admiralty. Six months later, in another letter appealing for funds, he wrote, 'If the *Implacable* is allowed to disappear we shall in a few years be building copies of her because no modern ship is so well designed'. The nation had saved the *Victory*, the Cobbs were preserving the *Foudroyant/ Trincomalee*; could not a third-rate be saved to complete the splendid series?

The Cobbs' financial difficulties worsened as the world economy spiralled into the Depression and industrial strife broke out in Britain's coalfields. Assistance almost materialised in 1924 when Sir James Caird, the Scottish shipping magnate who had contributed over £50,000 to the SNR's 'Save the *Victory*!' campaign, requested the Society's president Admiral Sir Charles Doveton Sturdee to investigate whether it was worth investing money in the training ship *Implacable*. Doveton Sturdee's initial enthusiasm was tempered by pessimistic reports from the marine surveyors and Caird, who was ready to donate up to £25,000 to the scheme, withdrew. However, after Sturdee's death Cobb contacted leading members of the SNR in 1925, including the editor of *Punch*, Sir Owen Seaman, asking them to reopen negotiations with Caird. After discussions, Sir James agreed to establish an endowment fund of £250 a year to cover the expense of training four boys annually in the Cobbs' ships.

The ships, however, continued to require large sums of money. In 1926 Cobb submitted his accounts to Caird with a request for further assistance. At that time the cost of maintaining the *Foudroyant* and *Implacable*, and servicing his debts, comprised almost half his annual expenditure of £10,883, and his bank overdraft had reached almost £15,000. Sir James sent an additional £2,000, but both men were aware that the *Implacable* in particular required yet another major overhaul which would cost tens of thousands. With Cobb in failing health, the SNR set up the *Implacable* Committee to take responsibility for the ship and to oversee her reconditioning. Key figures on the committee

were Sir Owen Seaman, who was elected chairman, Professor Geoffrey Callender, Secretary and Treasurer of the SNR, and later the first Director of the National Maritime Museum (NMM), Greenwich, and Colonel Harold Wyllie (son of the artist who had signed Cobb's 1909 petition). A public appeal led by Earl Beatty raised £25,000 - of which Caird donated £15,000 - and by 1927 the necessary repair work on *Implacable* was completed in Devonport.

However, rows with Falmouth Harbour Board over moorings forced Cobb to move the *Foudroyant* to Pembroke Dock in 1931. Early that same year Cobb, visiting London, was knocked down by a taxi. He developed peritonitis, dying on Good Friday 1931 in a Pembroke nursing home. Anna Cobb subsequently gifted the *Foudroyant* to the committee. In April the Duke of York (the future King George VI), Patron of the SNR, inaugurated a new

appeal to carry on Cobb's work. Later that year the two ships were brought to Portsmouth where they were moored near the entrance to Fareham Creek.

Under the SNRs guidance the project was developed as a 'holiday' centre for boys and, for the first time, girls. The two ships offered what the *Implacable* Committee described as a 'holiday home to the sea-conscious youth of the nation who are not well-off'. Up to three hundred children could be accommodated at one time, sleeping in hammocks and 'living in messes as in a man-of-war'.

They performed tasks on the ship, attended lessons in naval history, went boating and swimming. Boy Scouts continued to visit the ships, and were now joined by Girl Guides. From all accounts holidays on the ships were an extremely enjoyable experience.

The end of *Implacable*

On the outbreak of war in September 1939 the holiday schemes were suspended. Portsmouth was heavily bombed during the conflict, with hundreds of civilians killed and large areas of the city and dockyard reduced to rubble. Throughout the war both HMS *Victory* and the *Implacable* continued to serve the Royal Navy, the *Victory* as the flagship of the Commander-in-Chief at Portsmouth, the *Implacable*, recommissioned, as a training vessel and as a floating storage depot for bulk cargoes, especially coal.

By 1945 the two veterans of Trafalgar had survived yet another war but inevitably required additional expenditure. For the SNR the rescue of HMS *Victory* proved difficult enough, especially as there was tension with the Admiralty over the question of returning the ship to its status as a public attraction. The *Implacable*, meanwhile, was in a desperate state, her timbers rotting away. During the war the committee had inevitably lost its momentum and this lack of continuity left the ship in Portsmouth Harbour until 1947 when the Admiralty announced, yet again, that *Implacable* was to be disposed of.

Attempts were made by Harold Wyllie and Frank Carr - the latter a member of the SNR, and from 1947 successor to Callender as Director of the NMM - to revive the *Implacable* Committee. In October 1947 Carr suggested to the trustees of the Museum that the *Implacable* could be repaired, restored and re-rigged prior to finding a permanent berth at Greenwich as 'London's Trafalgar Ship'. Sir James Caird, since 1928 a trustee of the NMM, indicated that he might fund such a rescue project. Marine surveyors' reports, however, estimated costs around £150,000, with a further £50,000 required for re-rigging, and additional costs for ongoing maintenance. Caird would not countenance such enormous sums. He also warned his fellow trustees against launching a public appeal; for if it failed - as seemed likely in the austere economic conditions of post-war Britain - the loss of the *Im-*

DAILY GRAPHIC
and Daily Sketch
WEDNESDAY, NOVEMBER 27, 1946 ✳ A KEMSLEY NEWSPAPER FOUNDED IN 1890 1d.

VICEROY CALLED TO LONDON
Cabinet Move To End India Crisis—BACK PAGE

One Of England's 'Wooden Walls' Bids The Navy Good-bye
The Navy's oldest ship afloat, the wooden-hulled Implacable, which fought against Nelson at Trafalgar and was taken as a prize of war, lies up in Fareham Creek, Portsmouth, alongside the frigate Foudroyant. The Implacable has been the cradle of sailors for nearly a century, but she is due to pay off shortly and will cease to function as an Admiralty training establishment.

The end of Empire.
A year after the end of the Second World War the news of Implacable's *decommissioning coincides with calls in India for independence, in this front page from the* Daily Graphic, *27 November 1946.*

cable

Above: *The final voyage.*
The tug Alligator *towing the* Implacable *out of Portsmouth harbour to her final resting place in the Channel.*

Right: *The unkindest cut.*
In 1949, with the decision to scuttle the Implacable *announced, speed was essential to salvage her ornamental features. Here, dockyard workers remove the figurehead, later transported to Greenwich along with the pieces of the ship's stern.*

placable would be laid at their door. Reluctantly the trustees agreed. Other bodies were approached including the London County Council, Greenwich Borough Council, the Royal Commission on Historic Monuments, and the Georgian Group, all of whom had expressed interest in the project. Carr also secured the backing of Prince Philip, and the Prime Minister, Clement Attlee. But these organisations and individuals understandably balked at taking on responsibility for the vessel when informed that it might take anything up to half a million pounds to restore and maintain her. Eventually, the committee admitted defeat. A century-and-a-half after the *Duguay-Trouin*'s keel had been laid down at Rochefort, the ship had come to the end of her career.

The Admiralty gave to the NMM the figurehead and as much of the ornamental stern as could be removed, but that was all that could be saved. On Friday 2 December 1949 the *Implacable* - ballasted with scrap iron, primed with explosive charges, and bearing the flags of both the British and the French navies - was towed from Portsmouth on her last voyage. On the way out of the harbour she passed the aircraft carrier HMS *Implacable* (1942), the third ship to bear that name (the second being the battleship launched in 1895). Nine miles south of the Owers Lightship the old *Implacable* was anchored and the charges detonated. Unfortunately the Admiralty, anxious to make a good job of the sinking, had doubled the charges, and the subsequent explosion blew the bottom out of the ship, sending the ballast to the sea-bed but leaving the upper works afloat, with British and French ensigns still flying in the winter wind.

The distinguished spectators stayed until evening but had to leave the disintegrating remains drifting in the Channel, a hazard to shipping. A few days later wreckage from the *Implacable* washed up on the coast of France, some of it not far from Rochefort where she had first set sail.

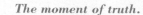

The moment of truth.
At 1.45 p.m. on 2 December 1949, with Implacable's hull, ballasted with 400 tons of pig-iron, the scuttling charges were exploded. Frank Carr described 'a cloud of smoke and debris' after which the vessel began to sink. Colours were at half-mast, the bugler sounded the Last Post. 'Then followed something of a contretemps, not to say a fiasco', Carr continued. 'Instead of the vessel completely foundering, she seemed to linger on with the top deck awash, and this went on for some hours...the White and French ensigns...continued to fly bravely, stubbornly and it seemed defiantly, long after the spectators had left the scene and turned for home. Later in the evening it was reported that the last of the wreck had disintegrated.'

The decision to sink *Implacable* had been taken in the context of post-war reconstruction, when Britain could scarcely afford to repair bomb damaged towns and cities, let alone old sailing ships. As the event receded, however, the realisation of what had taken place gradually spread. 'Never again', wrote Frank Carr, who witnessed the sinking, 'would human eyes see a line-of-battle ship under way'. Saving ships was still a minority pursuit but the enthusiasts, bruised from their battle to rescue the *Implacable*, at last began to organise their resistance on a world-wide scale. The major breakthrough came in the 1950s with the preservation of the *Cutty Sark*, a scheme led by Frank Carr and Prince Philip, and backed by an international fund-raising campaign. In 1970 the Maritime Trust was formed in Britain. The model of this organisation was taken up abroad and these disparate efforts were brought together in 1979 with the founding of the World Ship Trust, which adopted as its emblem a badge carrying an image of the *Implacable*'s stern and the motto '*Implacable*, Never Again'.

At present the Trust has over 1,300 vessels - ranging from sailing ships to submarines - on its register of historic ships, over a third of which are being 'actively restored' by groups of volunteers funded by state departments, national lotteries, individual patronage or public appeals. Once criticised for its temerity in seeking to rescue a small number of craft, the preservation movement as a whole is now more open to criticism for attempting to save every ship which is due for disposal. However, as the Trust has pointed out on numerous occasions 'Never Again' did not and does not mean that every ship due for destruction should be rescued. Even the *Implacable*, it is conceded, had been beyond repair by 1949, but swifter action and greater vigilance might have saved her. What the Trust emphasises is that no 'historically important' ship (a term that has to be continually reassessed) should ever again be destroyed if preservation is possible and if the means for it exist.

Crowning glory.
Implacable's stern, *taking pride of place overlooking*
Neptune Court, *the National Maritime Museum's*
Heritage Lottery-funded *project, which was*
completed in March 1999.

Resurfacing

The salvaged portions of *Implacable* have remained at Greenwich since 1950, when Sir James Caird paid £300 to have them brought from Portsmouth to the NMM. The figurehead was first put on display shortly after the ship's destruction. Plans were also laid for the carved stern - removed in haste and thus in pieces - to be reassembled and exhibited. Visitors entering the Museum would find themselves inside a replica of *Implacable*'s main stern cabin, with the poop deck forming a gallery for the display of Trafalgar relics. This proved too expensive, however, and the pieces of the stern remained in store. In 1960 these plans were revived as part of a scheme to develop Neptune Hall, a display space which had once been a school gymnasium, and in which the Museum, since 1937, had exhibited large ship models, figureheads and historic small craft. But again the stern carvings remained in storage, partly due to lack of funds but also because the Museum chose to display the paddle-tug *Reliant* (1907) in Neptune Hall instead.

It was not until 1991 that the stern was thoroughly surveyed. This time each piece was laid out, catalogued, photographed and measured. The new display plans for Neptune Hall and the surrounding galleries in 1993 meant that *Implacable*'s stern once again became a live issue. Ultimately the Heritage Lottery Fund provided a substantial grant to carry out the development of Neptune Hall - now Neptune Court - to coincide with the Millennium celebrations at Greenwich. Hempel's Marine Paints, Denmark, generously provided funds for the conservation and display of the stern and the figurehead.

Taken out of store, the pieces of the stern were painstakingly reassembled with the help of original plans drawn in 1810 at Plymouth dockyard and photographs of the ship, all of which are now in the Museum's collections. Missing sections were recarved using the original parts as templates, although the NMM, committed to maintaining the integrity of what remained, was determined to replicate as little as possible. After treatment to protect them from atmospheric degradation, the original carvings were simply given a coat of reversible isolating varnish. The Medusa figurehead, repainted and regilded, now looks out across a new Museum incorporating sixteen new galleries and displays on exploration, modern sea trade, passenger travel, marine art, ecology, maritime-inspired fashion and many other subjects.

Two hundred years after the launching of the *Implacable* her restored stern and figurehead greet a new century, in which the preservation of old ships will continue as a major heritage activity, owing much to the history and final fate of the *Implacable* herself. The ship's complete survival would have been preferable, but what remains is both a striking memorial and a reminder of her importance in the development of historic ship preservation as a whole.

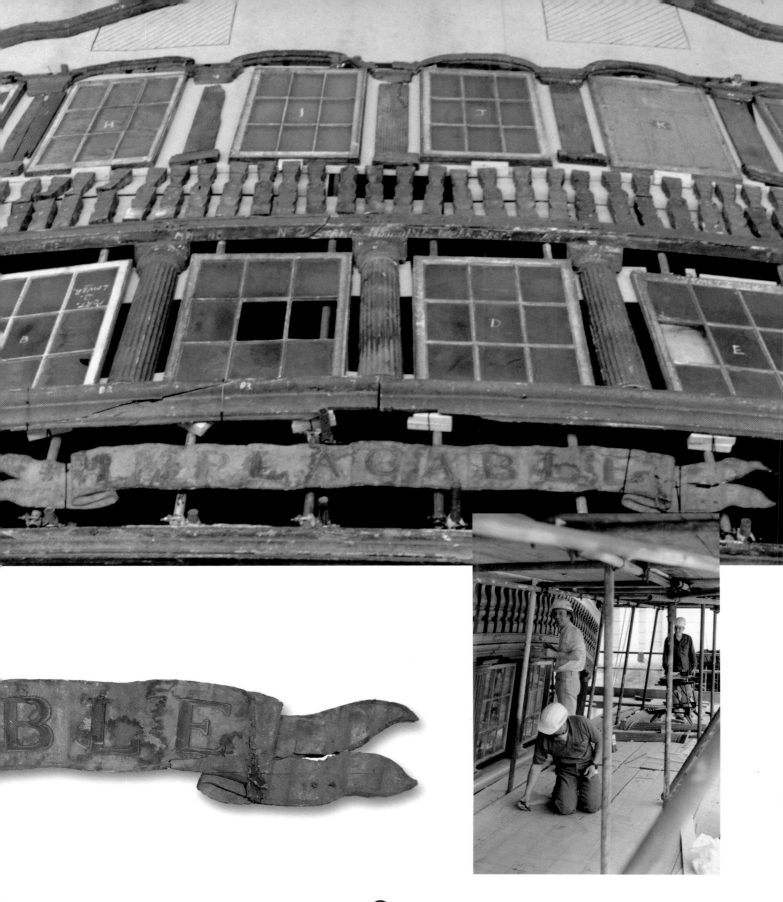

Acknowledgements

*The text was researched and written by Beverley Butler
and Kevin Littlewood.*

*The authors wish to thank the staffs of the following
institutions and organisations for assistance and
advice; the British Library; the National Maritime
Museum, Greenwich; the Public Record Office, Kew;
the Scout Association; Stratford Library, London;
University College London.*

Guide to further reading and research

Primary Sources

Information on the Implacable *in particular and the
preservation of old ships in general is available in the
archives of the National Maritime Museum, Greenwich.
Especially useful for the* Implacable's *history are the
records of the Society for Nautical Research (SNR),
housed in the NMM, and the correspondence between
Sir James Caird, G. W. Cobb and Sir Geoffrey Callender. Two important articles by Brian D. Price (Western
Telegraph, 22 and 29 July 1987) provide accounts of
Cobb and his projects drawn from contemporary
newspapers and from reminiscences of a Foudroyant
cadet.*

Secondary Sources

(Place of publication is London, unless otherwise stated)
The Story of the Implacable *(no author, no date, ?1938)*
Norman J Brouwer (ed.), International Register of
Historic Ships *(2nd ed., Oswestry, 1993).*
Frank Carr, 'Requiescat; HMS Implacable: *2 December
1949', in* The Mariner's Mirror, *Vol. 36, No. 2, April
1950 (pp. 107-110). G. E. W. Cobb,* A Trafalgar Ship for
Sea Scouts, An Appeal *(no date, ?1920)*
Encyclopaedia Britannica *(11th edition, Cambridge
1911), entry for Trouin, René Duguay. Clement Jones,*
Sea Trading and Sea Training *(1936) J. Michael Jones,*
Historic Warships *(Jefferson, N.C., 1993) Kevin Little-
wood and Beverley Butler,* Of Ships and Stars; Maritime
Heritage and the founding of the National Maritime Mu-
seum, Greenwich *(1998) A. J. Marsh,* The Story of a
Frigate, HMS Trincomalee to TS Foudroyant
(Portsmouth 1973).
The Times, *1892-1924, passim*
Country Life, *April -Aug. 1924, passim.*

National Maritime Museum Information

The National Maritime Museum is the largest maritime museum in the world. Its collections include manuscripts and rare books, 2,500 ship models, 4,000 paintings, 50,000 charts and 750,000 ship plans with hundreds of scientific and navigational instruments, chronometers, globes and large holdings of decorative and applied art.

The Museum also includes the Queen's House and the Royal Observatory, Greenwich. The Observatory is a short walk from the Museum through Greenwich Park.

Opening Times: 10.00-17.00 hrs daily, last admission 16.30 hours. Closed 24-26 December inclusive. CCTV is in operation in all galleries. Please do not touch the exhibits. No dogs (except assistance dogs). Smoking, eating and drinking are not allowed in the galleries. Photography is not permitted inside the buildings or on the site. Please check in advance for changes to opening dates and times by calling the NMM bookings unit on 0181 312 6608 or e-mail: bookings@nmm.ac.uk.

For general enquiries please contact:
National Maritime Museum, Greenwich, London SE10 9NF
Tel: 0181 858 4422, Fax: 0181 312 6632
or visit the National Maritime Museum web-site:
http://www.nmm.ac.uk

Centre for Maritime Research
The Centre for Maritime Research at the National Maritime Museum provides unrivalled access to this major UK collection.

Conferences and Seminars
For programme information please call: 0181 312 6616 or e-mail research@nmm.ac.uk.

Film Archive
The Museum's film archive houses more than 1,000 films dating back to 1910. For more information please call 0181 312 6645 or e-mail: lhillary@nmm.ac.uk or kjcost@nmm.ac.uk.

Film Location Services
The combined sites of the National Maritime Museum and the Royal Observatory, Greenwich, provide unique, elegant and historic locations for filming. For more information please call 0181 312 6710 or e-mail lhillary@nmm.ac.uk or kjcost@nmm.ac.uk.

Historic Photographs
The Museum's historic photograph collection contains the country's finest maritime photographs. For more information or to place an order please call 0181 855 1647.

Manuscripts and the Caird Library
Library opening times are Monday-Friday 10.00-16.45hrs.
For general information and details of Saturday opening times, please call: 0181 312 6672. For specific Library enquiries please e-mail: rxmack@nmm.ac.uk. For specific manuscript collection enquiries please e-mail: cxpowe@nmm.ac.uk.

Maps and Charts
The hydrography and cartography collections contain a large number of printed charts, atlases and sailing directions. A reproduction service is available. For more information please call 0181 312 6567 or e-mail: lhillary@nmm.ac.uk.

The Open Museum ® provides a programme of lectures and talks run in conjunction with Goldsmiths College, University of London. These explore diverse topics from aspects of the sea and shipping, to time, astronomy and navigation, local history and the arts. For a free prospectus telephone 0181 312 6747 or e-mail: cstevens@nmm.ac.uk.

Picture Library
There are more than 400,000 pictures comprising more than 4,000 oil paintings from the 17th to the 20th century, 50,000 prints and drawings and over 40,000 other images from the Museum's collection. For more information or to place an order please call 0181 312 6504 or e-mail: lxpring@nmm.ac.uk.

Port
'Port' is the Museum's subject-based information gateway on the Internet, dedicated to maritime studies. Access Port at: http://www.port.nmm.ac.uk

Research Enquiry Service
A fee paid research service is available to anyone who is unable to visit the Centre for Maritime Research. At the Royal Observatory, Greenwich, subject specialists offer expertise in the fields of astronomy and navigation, hydrography, horology and scientific instruments.
For more information please call: 0181 312 6712/6607/6727 or e-mail: lxveri@nmm.ac.uk.

Research Fellowships
For more information please call 0181 312 6559 or e-mail: research@nmm.ac.uk.

Search Station
The Search Station is a new multi-media resource which provides computerised access to highlights from the Museum's collections. Open to all visitors, schoolchildren and researchers. School parties by appointment only. Saturdays by appointment only. Closed bank holidays and third week in February. For more information please call: 0181 312 6616 or e-mail: research@nmm.ac.uk.

Education
The Education and Interpretation Department offers programmes and resources for schools, linked to the National Curriculum and GCSE. There are events to suit all ages, from the Crowsnest Club which provides activities for the youngest visitors to specialist gallery talks and tours. For more information please call 0181 312 6608 or e-mail: bookings@nmm.ac.uk.

Events
The National Maritime Museum offers a wealth of entertainment opportunities in the heart of Greenwich. For more information on entertaining at the National Maritime Museum, Royal Observatory and Queen's House please call the Events Office on 0181 312 6674/6693 or e-mail: lacook@nmm.ac.uk.

Friends of the National Maritime Museum
Membership includes free entry with a guest to all Museum galleries, a Friends Room, a full programme of events at home and abroad and Friends' magazines. For more information please call 0181 312 6632 or visit the National Maritime Museum web-site.

Restaurant and Café
The Restaurant and Café are open during normal opening hours. The Café provides a quick and convenient quality snack and beverage service for visitors. The Restaurant offers a more comprehensive morning, lunch-time and afternoon menu.

Shopping
Imaginative gifts which reflect the wealth of the Museum's collections. In addition to two shops on site, purchases can be made via mail order and the National Maritime Museum web-site. Please call 0181 312 6700 or e-mail: hxmath@nmm.ac.uk.

Sponsorship
For information on how to become involved in the development programme please contact the Head of Corporate Development, National Maritime Museum on 0181 312 6701 or e-mail: hjbeio@nmm.ac.uk.

Visitors with Disabilities
The Museum is committed to the development of facilities for disabled visitors. Flat access is via the North Entrance. There are specialist programmes, large print guides, touch packs and audio guides available from the Information Desk. Please call 0181 312 6608 or e-mail: bookings@nmm.ac.uk.